To Maria,
    Live in the don't stay in the past & don't worry about the future as it hasn't happened yet.
    Much love

2017

I Am Still Me

A Collection of Poems

Tracey Shorthouse

authorHOUSE®

AuthorHouse™ UK
1663 Liberty Drive
Bloomington, IN 47403 USA
www.authorhouse.co.uk
Phone: 0800.197.4150

© 2017 Tracey Shorthouse. All rights reserved.

No part of this book may be reproduced, stored in a retrieval system, or transmitted by any means without the written permission of the author.

Published by AuthorHouse 02/06/2017

ISBN: 978-1-5246-6819-8 (sc)
ISBN: 978-1-5246-6820-4 (hc)
ISBN: 978-1-5246-6821-1 (e)

Print information available on the last page.

Any people depicted in stock imagery provided by Thinkstock are models, and such images are being used for illustrative purposes only.
Certain stock imagery © Thinkstock.

This book is printed on acid-free paper.

Because of the dynamic nature of the Internet, any web addresses or links contained in this book may have changed since publication and may no longer be valid. The views expressed in this work are solely those of the author and do not necessarily reflect the views of the publisher, and the publisher hereby disclaims any responsibility for them.

Contents

I'm Still Me 1
Ode to a Nurse 3
Prison of Thoughts 6
Love and Life 9
Meditation 12
The Tree of Life 15
Independence Day 17
Remembering The Past 19
Missing Me 21
Why? 24
The Music Box 26
Seasons of the Heart 31
Reborn 34
The Spirit Guide 36
Dementia and Me 39
Contours of my Mind 42
Windmills 44
Today 46
Music Memories 48
Lost Memories 50
Love 52
The Magical Forest 54
My Garden 56
Ode to Casper 58
Acceptance 61
Walking in the Woods 63
The Sensory Garden 66

The Pirate Sonnet 69
The Fortune Teller 71
Wishing 76
AUTUMN 78
Rushing 80
The Halloween Party 82
Our Nan 85
Christmas Thoughts 87
Dear Santa 88
The Christmas Fairy 90

This book is dedicated to my family and friends who have encouraged me so much since my diagnosis. Especially Bobbie Ann Carr who first encouraged me to start writing in the first place.

I was diagnosed with Early Onset of Alzheimer's Disease and Posterior Cortical Atrophy in December 2015. I cope with having this by being optimistic and positive, and by being vocal about dementia. It's not a case of it being shoved under the carpet or not being spoke about like it used to. How else can we learn if not open about it? I do a variety of things to get out there and keep my brain active which is the most important thing including talks. This is why I have decided to write this book, to prove to others that just because you have a condition doesn't mean that you have to give up. I never wrote poetry before I had dementia and now I write all the time.

The book is called I Am Still Me because I haven't changed personality since having dementia even though I did lose a lot of friends in the beginning.

I'm Still Me

I'm still me, despite the dementia,
Ready for the new adventure,
Still optimistic, positive and happy
knowing there is still time for me to meet a new chappie.

To recall or recognise is sometimes hard,
So maybe I need some special cards,
However, all this does not make me mad,
Not even bad or sometimes sad.

I might forget that two and two is four at times,
But at least I don't succumb to any crimes,
I also have the concentration of a gnat,
But I still have the company of a cat.

Casper is his name,
And he loves me just the same,
I might not be able to drive now,
But there are other ways to travel somehow.

I might worry about what was and what is,
But at least my hair is still a frizz,
I might not have dinner parties anymore,
But then, who is keeping score.

I still bake, garden and do crafts,
And still enjoy a few laughs,
With friends and family who keep in touch,
Sometimes we go out and go Dutch.

I like to walk and mooch in the zone,
With the help of my trusty phone,
When the maps and GPS come into place,
This all helps me, to save some face.

So, what if my speech is affected
There is no course for me to be rejected,
So, there you see, that I'm still me
And there is no need for you to flee.

Ode to a Nurse

Back in the day, when I first started nursing
Old Flo and Edith were my idols
Sometimes the training made me start cursing
But we were always given a couple of Bibles

I always wanted to be like Flo with her lamp
Giving care where it was needed
But I am glad that our wards were never damp
But at least with her, knowledge was seeded

I always thought Edith Cavell was so brave
Saving the men as she did,
Her life for her country she gave
Because of the soldiers she hid

I always loved being a nurse
Giving those poorly the gentle touch
Being there if they got worse
Giving of myself a little too much

A hand on a fevered brow
An ear to listen to
Making sure that they had plenty of chow
And giving tissues and hugs to those who were really blue

Tracey Shorthouse

I used to always treat each one of my patients
As if they were my own flesh and blood
Having the really poorly patients near the nursing stations
In case, they fell out of bed and caused a thud

As nurses, we are either at the beginning of life, at the birth
Or at the end, when someone's live is ebbing away
But wherever they are on the spectrum of life, they still have their worth
Then tomorrow is still another day

Sometimes I saw the worse that people could do each other
Or the worse they could do to themselves
At times, there were those who would call out for their mother
Maybe in time, we could take care of ourselves

Although I enjoyed being on the ward
I much preferred being out in the district
I never ever got bored
And still remained optimistic

We only see a small window of people's lives in hospital
And understand a lot more out and about
There is plenty of time to be philosophical
Although sometimes patients still shout

But you have to understand, they don't mean to be nasty
Sometimes they are in pain, or just a little fed up
Sometimes their wounds can be ghastly
But they will always offer you a cup

Sometimes I used to do more than I should
Like make a cup of tea, or feed their cat
But it was always for something good
And I always fitted in a little chat

I Am Still Me

So now I have retired,
And the past is now the past
Although I feel like I may have expired
But I at least I know that I had a blast

You can't take those memories
I know I was a good nurse
My life is full of treasuries
And now I just keep writing a verse

Tracey Shorthouse

Prison of Thoughts

Let me out, let me out
Can you not see inside the contours of my mind?
Why do you have to doubt?
Why do you feel the need to bind?

The corridors are long and winding
Full of space and yet locked doors
I feel cross that you are so binding
As I run across the floors

I bang on the windows, and then the doors
Racing back and forth
I search frantically through my drawers
Then back to East, West, South and North

All you do is make me anxious
I so want to be free
My mind should be a blank canvas
But it's not, so I will shout and I will plea

Let me out, let me out right now
You can't keep me prisoner
You promised and made a vow
But all you have done is imprison her

I Am Still Me

Her is me, don't you hear?
It's so unfair, this prison of walls
When you are there and I am here
You say it is to prevent my falls

Why have you put me in this place?
Full of locks and bars
I spend my life pacing within the space
But as I peer out, I see all the cars

I want so much to be free
Like a bird gliding through the sky
Or like the fish in the sea
Yet all I do is sit and cry

As I am here within the confinements of the home
And the prison of my mind
Where I am allowed to roam
And the nurses here are so kind

Don't forget that I miss you, child
For that is how I remember you
You used to be so wild
Even more as you grew

Please let me come home with you
I promise that I will be good
I will make you my famous stew
You told me that you would if you could

But that I will be too unsafe to leave
My mind doesn't understand
I wiped my face on my sleeve
Then you gave me a reprimand

And gave me a tissue instead
You sighed and looked at your watch
I felt there was a lot things unsaid
Yet I couldn't remember, so asked if you still did the hopscotch

I don't remember you leaving
And here am I pacing again
Why is everyone so deceiving
Why doesn't anyone explain?

Love and Life

The old lady sat at her dressing table mirror
Brushing her hair stroke after stroke
The image of herself got clearer and clearer
The threat of tears she managed to choke

Who she is, who cares to remember
When she looks, she is a gay young thing
Favourite month has always been September
And she always, always loved to sing

With faraway eyes, she continues to brush
A secret smile appears on her lips
She always had more than one crush
But her heart belonged to one on the ships

A young sailor was he, and she caught his eye,
As he came upon the shore one day
First date was a picnic under a blue sky
Then he went and proposed sometime in May

Her family were pleased and happy
As he had good prospects in the Navy
He was so good, kind and never snappy
And his hair was always very wavy

The old lady stopped brushing for a second
A blush tinged her cheeks
She remembered how he used to beckon
How they both used to enjoy reaching those peaks

When they used to make love to each other
His touch and kisses were so sweet
He totally loved her, but wasn't one to smother
But nor was he ever one too cheat

The old lady resumed the brushing, more gently this time
A single tear rolled down her cheek
In her mind, she could hear the bells of her clock chime
When war broke out, it was her worst week

As soon as war was declared, they both knew
That the Navy would definitely be involved
She did everything she could not to get blue
And prayed that everything would soon get resolved

Off he went to fight the great fight
But soon a telegram came
It came in the dead of the night
And there in black letters was his name

She felt like an explosion had hit her chest
And wondered if anyone could die of a broken heart
She placed a hand on her breast
And felt the tears start to smart

He was killed in action so the telegram said
At least he suffered no pain
It was the one thing she always used to dread
Being alone without her Wayne

I Am Still Me

She placed a hand on her tummy
Thinking of the life that was starting there
Knowing that soon she will be a mummy
And there was already waiting a little stuffed bear

A boy named Tommy was born
Looked the splitting image of his dad
But there really wasn't time to mourn
And he grew up to be a good lad

And the cycle of life goes on
Memories that started to appear now fade
The long curtains have now been drawn
The old lady gets on her knees and prayed

She prays for the life she has had,
For the spirits that haunt her dreams
For her family and her lad
Sometimes she feels like the cat who has got the creams

The old lady climbs into bed
And pulls the covers up to her chin
And remembers when she was wed
And the honeymoon at the inn

Sleep and death come together
Her man then comes to meet her
With a spray of beautiful heather
Together their spirits become a blur.

Tracey Shorthouse

Meditation

When you go for a walk
What do we you see?
Shall you see a hawk?
Shall you walk by the quay?

Do you like the sound of water?
Or the trees whispering?
Maybe you will see an otter
Or feel a bee sting

Stop for a moment
And close your eyes
Smell the scent
And hear the birds cry

How relaxing do you feel
Knowing you are safe
If you want, you can kneel
And you won't get a chafe

Breath slowly and deeply
Taking in the sounds
You may feel dreamy
But there are no bounds

I Am Still Me

Sometimes this is how you meditate
Drifting in your mind
Never feeling any hate
And not your teeth to grind

Or you can physically go out and about
Wherever you find peace
And this will leave no other doubt
That all anguish shall then cease

It's so important to let things go
To relax as life is too short
This will cause your energies to flow
Although I know some people like to use sport

As a means for relaxation
Like yoga and tai chi
This goes across the nation
And it's a natural way to be free

So, find your happy medium
Of whatever you want to do
Maybe listen to the drums
Or walk past the yews

But take at least 10 – 15 minutes
Out of your day
As this will increase your inner fitness
And will make you feel gay

Go for a walk
Take in the sights
Don't take a clock
Make sure you see some kites

Tracey Shorthouse

As they are beautiful birds
Do you not know
These are the end of my little words
Just remember to go nice and slow

The Tree of Life

The tree stood steadfast and tall
In the middle of a field
The wind would occasionally blow up a squall
Yet the branches refused to yield

It had been there for many years
And had been hit by all weathers
At times the field had been full of corn ears
And other times purple heathers

Yet this tree continued to breathe life
From the roots, up to the branches
And even when kids carve their names with a knife
It continues to stand tall and staunches

The warmth of the sun brings
Positivity to its soul
Although the trees age is shown through its rings
This doesn't stop the mole

From appearing under the soil
Which helps feed the roots
And nothing then will spoil
Those brand-new shoots

Then the rain will come
Adding another value to life
Sometimes the sap can cause a kind of gum
And the farmer is due to take a wife

The air that we breathe has a way
To communicate with the tree
In making the branches sway
And the blossoms in spring will attract the bee

When the leaves start to drop
Under the tree covering the ground
And the farmer has pulled the last of his crop
And the birds make that sound

Of sweet music to your ears
Tweeting away their cares
And slowly the years
Go past, and so do the hares

And there it is, the tree of life
Standing there season after season
Seeing all sorts of strife
Sometimes beyond all reason

Independence Day

Happy Fourth of July,
To my American Friends
Fly the flag under the blue sky
Think of those men, who used the pens

To draft the Declaration of Independence
From the British Empire
Those five men who stood in tendance
But it didn't stop a fire

With the American Revolution
Which reigned from 1765 to 1783
There was an eventual resolution
Which ended with a plea

Thirteen American colonies there were
Who stood strong and unwavering
Knowing and went on to spur
Great Britain, who they now were disfavouring

King George sat on his throne
Read the Declaration with some disbelief
He probably let out a loud groan
Knowing he was no longer their chief

Tracey Shorthouse

He looked at the 56 names
From all the 13 colonies, there were
Chose to ignore the claims
Then everything was a blur

So, 4th July 1776 was a day in history
Which is always celebrated in style
There was never ever a mystery
Nor was it ever a trial

It is considered a national holiday
With fireworks, parades and fairs
And enough music to make you sway
And for you all to forget your cares

However, don't ever forget those
Who stood up for your beliefs
Those men who eventually chose
To become your many chiefs

Remembering The Past

Stand still and remember
The millions of lives that were lost
Armistice Day is in November
And there is always, always a cost

War is never a good thing
Cause people always die
Snipers cause a sting
Whereas spitfires rule the sky

Now we remember that D Day is in June
Here lies the Normandy Landings
The organisers checked the phase of the moon
To make sure that everyone was still standing

The Army, Navy and Air Force took control
Over land, sea and air
All three looking towards the same goal
To make and cause a scare

The Battle of the Somme is being remembered in July
This was considered the bloodiest
The men definitely needed an ally
Cause it was also considered the muddiest

The Battle of Britain is in September
When Winnie told us that "so much owed by so many to so few"
This is when we need to remember
Those special airmen who especially flew

We all remember the fight between Bismarck and Hood
All those lives lost at sea
But the Ark Royal did what she could
And saved the day with glee

Stand still and recall
See the poppies in the field
Knowing that time will heal all
And our land will also be healed

It saddens me that our men and women still go out to fight
To keep our country safe and free
All through the day and night
Over land, air and sea.

Such strong and fearless souls
Who sees such awful sights?
Working towards the same goals
Giving our enemies lots of frights

Missing Me

Sometimes I miss me, the old me
The girl who liked to go dancing
Now the music seems too loud
I used to spin around with glee
But at least I still love laughing
But I don't like to be part of the crowd

At times, the noise is too much for me to cope with
Like angry bees stuck in my head, buzzing constantly
I miss going out and about, being part of the crew
But at least I still believe in magic, spirit and myth
And I still believe in honestly
But sometimes I still get blue

I miss driving around, going to different places
And sometimes I do miss work, hard to believe
And I do miss my memory at times
But I still remember some faces
And it's not like me to grieve and grieve
Although my tastes have changed, I still like my limes

Tracey Shorthouse

I miss watching the dramas, but get lost easily
Sometimes it's hard for me to tell fiction from reality
Then I get scared which was never like me
But at least I live peacefully
And will always be free
And I am lucky that I live between the countryside and sea

I loved how I could see the changes of the seasons when out and about
And how the skies change depending on the weather
That was the best thing about being a community nurse
At least, not working means that there is no one left to shout
But who cares as long as we are together
And I am determined that the dementia will not get worse

As friends and family, we have each other's back
Although it is also nice to be that someone's special
Someone to see beyond and just see me
It's nice to be alone, but also nice to be part of a pack
But I also don't want to meet a devil
And I don't want to be seen to flee

I don't like the fact that I get tired
Or that my speech gets slurred
Or that I have to walk with a stick sometimes
It seems mad that I am admired
By some, my vision sometimes gets blurred
But now I have retired I now write rhymes

But on the upside, I am still able to walk
I still garden and explore different areas
By using public transport
Sometimes I have to steed myself as want to balk
But I try not to take myself too serious
And occasionally I still allow myself a glass of port

I Am Still Me

So, although I do miss the old me
I am getting used to this new person
I am still positive and full of beans
And can still make the odd stew
And I quite like this new version
Of me and my family genes

Why?

Why can't you just accept me for who I am?
I am no different from you
The way you perceive me, makes the dam
Want to burst, at your point of view

Why can't you just love me for me being me?
And not put me in your gilded cage
All I want to be is loved and free
Yet all you do is show me your rage

Why don't you listen, instead of running away?
Do you not think I deserve some love?
All I am asking for you is to trust and stay
We both need peace like a dove

Why are you so afraid, of something that is beyond our control?
Life is for living, and getting on with life
I am willing to love you and give you a bit of my soul
Not to carry on with this strife

Why can't I just meet a man of my dreams?
Someone who will love me no matter what
Someone who will walk with me alongside the streams
Someone who won't let me get stuck in that rut

I Am Still Me

Of what life can entail sometimes
Why do people fear what they cannot see?
You know that I am still in my prime
I am not here to sit and plea

We could all wish for this and that
And wonder why, what and when
If someone doesn't like where I am at
Then maybe I will just have to begin again

For one day, there will be someone who will accept me
Who will complete my life, no matter what
Then my life will be full of glee
There might be room for a cot, but there again maybe not

We all wish for that house with a picket fence
And two children at the most
But sometimes that doesn't make sense
As sometimes pets can be equally close

So, all I want is peace in my heart
Not to keeping asking why?
For I know that I am quite smart
And also, very spry

Tracey Shorthouse

The Music Box

In an empty house
At the edge of a forest
A sound of tinkering is heard
With the footsteps of the grouse
And the birds and their chorus
Everything else gets blurred

The birds stop their song
And the deer stop in their tracks
And the wind starts whistling down
The house has been empty that long
That anyone could see the cracks
If they ever came up from town

However, no one really ventures there
Stories of ghosts and spirits are rife
As the sound of music is often heard
Sometimes the boys go up for a dare
Even if their mothers find out and give them strife
The boys find it all a bit absurd

As they traipse through the fields to the house
With their torches, together they hold
An owl swoops down, and twigs snap under their feet
As they try to be as quiet as a mouse
Luckily the air isn't cold
But they still huddled together for some heat

The house stands still and bleak
A door swings on its hinges
And a gate bangs with the wind
Suddenly a fox starts to shriek
Making the boys start to cringe
And they were starting to feel like they had sinned

By being up there, against all the rules
But there was no backing out now
So they ventured forwards, pushing and shuffling
Feeling like a pack of fools
Wishing they had brought some chow
Making some noise with their bustling

They entered with some unease
And saw some stairs ahead
Up they went one by one
One of the boys stifled a sneeze
The carpet they saw used to be red
And they really wanted to run

But being brave and bold, and wanting to save some face
Onwards and upwards they carried on
Until they reached the attic
They spied, in the corner, a small case
One of the boys did a yawn
And nearly tripped over causing a small panic

Tracey Shorthouse

They looked at him and shushed him
He shrugged and rolled his eyes
The case was then opened and a small box was inside
They turned and looked at Tim
Since he was in charge, and this might be a prize
So, he took the box in his stride

As he held the box to see if he could open it
A sweet melody started, echoing throughout the house
They jumped and looked around
And really wanted to split
But the house seemed to start to rouse
Which made the boys frown

The box lifted its lid as if by magic
A silver little hammer was hitting a little disc
Which was spinning around and round
The sound started a little tragic
The boys knew they were taking a risk
But they still watched in wonder as the box got wound

On its own accord, the house became alive
With distant murmurs of voices past
And glasses clinked together, and laughter was heard
The house was no longer a dive
The moment seemed too last
And everything had stirred

The boys looked at each other in horror
And Tim dropped the box back into the case
And they turned and ran back down the stairs
They saw the house in full glory, but only saw the spirits aura
In one of the rooms, the fire was roaring in its place
The boys then saw tables and chairs

I Am Still Me

They stood on the stairs looking in awe
Feeling pretty scared but not really accepting
One by one the voices diminished and the music started to fade
The boys could not believe what they saw
They felt that the house was protecting
Itself, and really wanted to withdraw

The boys carried on down the stairs, and hit the door with a force
It no longer was off its hinges, but a solid mass it now was
They fell to the floor in a heap, grappling for the handle
Tim's voice had gone quite hoarse
He was wishing they hadn't broken the laws
And he suddenly felt like a vandal

He managed to turn the handle, and outwards they bundled
When they reached the gate, they turned
Silence reigned once more and the house was back in disarray
They looked at each other and without a word they trundled
Inside the house, the fire no longer burned
And the table and chairs had gone away

In the attic, the lid of the music box closed on its own
And invisible hands closed down the lid on the case
A breeze shifted things slightly, then nothing
Except the house's usual groan
Meanwhile the boys picked up the pace
All that could be heard was the sound of their puffing

As they were nearly out of breath, once they hit town
Tim stopped them from going further
And made them promise to keep silent
And always keep their heads down
Years later when he became a server
He remembered how one of them became violent

From having nightmares from being in the house
And not being able to talk about it
Although he felt guilty, he always felt that the house needed to be protected
And he never ever told his spouse
But often went up to the forest whenever he had the need to split
As he thought that somehow the house and he were connected

And he remembered the music box, and the melody that it spun
It was forever haunting his dreams
Although he could never quite pinpoint the lyrics
And he never even told his son
Although he had heard of a few schemes
To knock down the house, nothing could really disturb those old spirits

Seasons of the Heart

Can I go out and play, mama?
The snow has nearly gone
The little girl was still in her pyjamas
As it was turning dawn

She turned to look at her mother
Who was looking so pale and worn
Her father was bound to smother
His wife when she looked so drawn

Lucy sighed inwardly, and went and got dressed
She knew it wasn't her fault her mama was ill
She buttoned up her coat up to her breast
And pulled the sledge up the hill

As she sat on the sledge, going back down again
She emptied her mind and continued to play
It was only when there was a hint of rain
That she collected her things, then she heard a neigh

As she looked down the lane, she saw a horse and cart
She knew it was the doctor and Dobby
She felt the tears start to smart
By the time, she reached home, the doctor was in the lobby

He patted her head and lifted her chin
And told her how big she was getting
She gave him a thin grin
And left him as the table needed setting

Time went on, and soon it was Spring
New growth and changes were afoot
Lucy worried about what the new year would bring
As she sat under the tree with her book

Mama sat in the shade sleeping
Pills and potions on the table near by
The ivy was seen creeping
Around the house up to the sky

The air was still cool, and Lucy helped her mama inside
At times, she felt so very much alone
But she took everything in her stride
And she wasn't one to moan

Summer came and with it came heat
Mama sat outside more often
The fields were full of wheat
And the colours in the garden began to soften

Everything blended together, and the birds sang a song
Of good cheer, Even the frogs were happy
Lucy knew she had to be strong
As her father was apt to get a bit snappy

But this was only because he was tired
As mama rarely slept now, from being in pain
It was thankful that he was retired
As not working kept him sane

I Am Still Me

The leaves started to turn, and nights drew in
As Autumn reared her head
Lucy had started to cream Mama's skin
As by now it was so thin and always bled

Mama was in bed all the time now
Sleeping off and on
Lucy often soothed her fevered brow
The doctor warned them it wouldn't be long

Lucy was as quiet as a mouse in her room
Dad sat in the rocking chair next to the bed
And suddenly, she felt a sense of doom
When the news came that her mama was dead

Autumn turned to Winter, and the snow laid on the ground
When the family finally said their final goodbyes
The churchyard was devoid of sound
And Lucy whispered, "Goodbye Mama" up to the skies

A single tear trickled down her cheek
And a slight breeze was felt
A mouse scurried by and let out a squeak
The sun came out, and the snow started to melt

Tracey Shorthouse

Reborn

The universe is vast, full of empty space
The stars' twinkle and shine, yet they still die
But then they are reborn, through the mechanisms of life

No one really dies, yet no one really lives
There is silence yet there is noise
It is an enigma, that no one can really explain

We always think we have a greater understanding of things
Yet we really don't understand at all
We see, yet we really don't

We think we listen, yet do we?
Spirit is all around us, but we cannot see them
Although when we open ourselves, we might sense them

The world turns slowly on its axis,
Night turning to day, turning to night
Minutes, hours, seasons all rolling by

We are all reborn sooner or later
Like the stars in the sky
Like the pendulum of the clock that never stops

I Am Still Me

Tracey Shorthouse

The Spirit Guide

Look ahead and what do you see
Look at that swarm of bees
But do not feel alarm
For they mean you no harm

Look left and right
The sun is quite bright
The sky is blue
And there are plenty of hues

The trees are brown and green
And some are fat and lean
Wildflowers are everywhere
And the stream, beside you, is quite clear

Sit as the grass is so lush
And listen to the rush
Of the water going by
And just swat at that fly

This is what you need to do
To stop, when you are feeling blue
Smile and feel happy
And see the children clapping

I Am Still Me

For they are our past, present and future
And one day, life will need sutures
Against the fighting and strife
Which has become part of our life

We the spirits guide fear
That unless things become clear
Mankind will be gone
And this will feel furlong

That all our hard work will be in vain
But, I guess, that is the bane
Of being a guide
So, our charge can abide

Look at life with joy
Now don't be coy
We will always be there
As will the bears

Just ask and we will tell
Listen to the bells
Or any other calling card
Some might make it really hard

Just listen to your senses
And don't be tense
We will protect you
Just as a lamb is protected by an ewe

Tracey Shorthouse

Dementia and Me

Sometimes I think there is a race
Between my dementia and me
Although it is going at a slow pace
I still wish I was free

My memory used to be hot
Especially with knowledge and spelling
Now I am really not
My brain is its new dwelling

It is like having an alien residing in my brain
At times, it takes control
And I feel a lot of strain
As my memories unroll

What did happen yesterday or last week
I really don't remember
I sigh as everything looks bleak
Since I was diagnosed in December

I want to yell and scream
And tell it to go away
Maybe it is all a dream
But then again I know it will be okay

Because I am a fighter
And in control
And have become a writer
Even though I am not on a pay role

I retired as a nurse in May
Even now that is becoming a distant memory
But at least I can be gay
But the dementia still takes my energy

I hate feeling tired all the time
Having to pace myself
But I am still in my prime
Even though the books remain on the shelf

I miss reading and listening to music
Remembering and concentrating is really hard
But at least I am still lucid
And still write the odd card

My perception of things is often off
I stumble and my speech is sometimes slurred
I worry that people might then scoff
But at least my vision doesn't get blurred

Damn you dementia! I want to yell
I want to get cross and stamp my feet
But it is only a short spell
Then I feel a bit of a cheat

As the dementia has no voice
It can neither see or hear
And I know I have a choice
But sometimes I wish I was a seer

I Am Still Me

To see how long, I have before the dementia takes over
But I think I wish to live my life to the best of my ability
As I could never be a rover
And at least I prefer some tranquillity

So, although my life is a fight
Between the dementia and me
I will win just out of spite
And kick the dementia with glee

Tracey Shorthouse

Contours of my Mind

Please don't ever look deep into my eyes
As I fear of what you might see
There is only so much of a guise
I can pull over thee

I try and hide so much of what I am feeling
From you and everyone
You have no clue at what I am dealing
With, I fear that one day you might shun

Oh dear, why must we all think so much
For what others may think
I yearn for your touch
Yet, I also have the need to shrink

My mind is a two-way street
Full of joy and despair
But when I look back, my life has been no mean feat
At each moment, I have sent up a prayer

Even if you don't believe in Him
He will listen regardless, and always send love
I have always liked the odd hymn
Maybe the man I meet will fit like a glove

I Am Still Me

Sometimes in my mind's eye
I want to close myself off in a room
Curl myself up in a ball, away from the night's sky
And fill myself up with doom and gloom

Yet, I know that this isn't healthy
My mind needs joy and positive feelings
I don't need to be wealthy
Just a lot of laughter, and to hear some squealing's

As this comes mostly from children
Or when lovers chase each other, before one is caught
Love should conquer in every building
And overpower every negative thought

So when you look into my eyes
Hopefully all you see is love and kindness
There won't be negativity or lies
Just lots of colour and no blindness

Tracey Shorthouse

Windmills

Sometimes I feel like a mechanical toy,
That has been wound up in the morning
I feel bouncing and full of joy
And I never get any warning

When suddenly, in the afternoon
I start to slow down and falter
There doesn't have to be a full moon
And I don't have to be near the water

My mind is sometimes never my own
It feels like it is full of windmills
I feel slightly out of my zone
When I get tired, it gives me the chills

My mind is turning, but never getting anywhere
Wanting to scramble, looking for knowledge
I often look up and send a prayer
Which is sometimes often acknowledged

Sometimes I feel that all I see and hear is white noise
The more I try to understand, the more tired I get
Hence why I sometimes feel like one of the toys
And sometimes I really start to fret

I Am Still Me

Please someone, can you just wind me up?
As I know that I will be okay
Just give me a minute and a cup
Then I can make some headway

You know that I am still me, don't you?
I haven't really changed, as still the same
I am still the person that you knew
I just can't always remember your name

Please, please don't go away and leave me
Just remember that all I do is need to be wound
I don't mean to sit here and plea
But then I can get going and I'm not so bound

By life, and my mind is my own
This alien hasn't taken over just yet
You will never hear me groan and moan
Nor will I ever be in debt

Today

Today is a fresh day
Where we can make a clean start
Try to be happy and gay
And always do things from the heart

Spread a little kindness along your way
For no pay in return
And maybe you will hear the sound of the jay
Or the whispers of the fern

The orange blossom spreads her scent
As do the roses
They are the best in Kent
And also make good posies

Many people hope to find pots of gold
At the end of every rainbow
However, the stories of that are fairly old
But at least the colours then do glow

The early morning mists shroud round
Like the town of Brigadoon
The birds make their sound
Whilst couples start their honeymoon

I Am Still Me

Please someone, can you just wind me up?
As I know that I will be okay
Just give me a minute and a cup
Then I can make some headway

You know that I am still me, don't you?
I haven't really changed, as still the same
I am still the person that you knew
I just can't always remember your name

Please, please don't go away and leave me
Just remember that all I do is need to be wound
I don't mean to sit here and plea
But then I can get going and I'm not so bound

By life, and my mind is my own
This alien hasn't taken over just yet
You will never hear me groan and moan
Nor will I ever be in debt

Today

Today is a fresh day
Where we can make a clean start
Try to be happy and gay
And always do things from the heart

Spread a little kindness along your way
For no pay in return
And maybe you will hear the sound of the jay
Or the whispers of the fern

The orange blossom spreads her scent
As do the roses
They are the best in Kent
And also make good posies

Many people hope to find pots of gold
At the end of every rainbow
However, the stories of that are fairly old
But at least the colours then do glow

The early morning mists shroud round
Like the town of Brigadoon
The birds make their sound
Whilst couples start their honeymoon

I Am Still Me

Be wise and safe in what you do
Forget about tomorrow
Don't let the past haunt you
And let the cobwebs blow

Tracey Shorthouse

Music Memories

Music is the essence of the soul
At certain times it can bring back memories
Sometimes when you take a stroll
Your mind is full of treasuries

I always wake up with a song in my head
Full of laughter and cheer
There is never any dread
My mind is actually quite clear

Sometimes it is a song of distant past
That comes into mind
It's funny how these songs last
Sometimes they are one of a kind

Like the family songs that no one has ever heard of
Whoever knew that Uncle Jim has a red nose
But at least these are remembered with love
And there are at least three verses to this prose

Some songs remind me when I was a child
Songs that dad played a lot
We were never all that wild
Although there are some songs that should have been shot

I Am Still Me

I like almost anything
Any music that there is
Elvis was always seen as the king
But I could never win a quiz

I love all the old music
Know all the words
At least I am still lucid
Might be seen to be one of the nerds

Classical, Country, Jazz and blues
All come into mind
But whatever genre that you choose
Depending on what you find.

Forties, fifties and sixties
Are always the best
We could be like gypsies
And be truly blessed

Can't beat The Platters
Or the Rat Pack
But all it is that matters
That you know that you won't get any flak

You are very lucky if you know the words
To the old Music Hall Songs
You don't have to be known to the herds
And they won't get any gongs

So be still and relax
Let the music wash over you
Listen to the tracks
And never get blue

Tracey Shorthouse

Lost Memories

Who am I, I know not
I now can't remember
I feel like I may have lost the plot
When is December?

Who are you? I should know
Your eyes look at me knowing
Yet they are also full of woe
When will it start snowing?

These are random thoughts, I know
But my mind is so muddled
Look how those flowers grow
Sometimes I feel like I am fuddled

I look at you, trying to remember
Let's go for a walk
Is your birthday in November?
Let us try to talk

You grab my hand and I freeze
And offer my arm instead
There is a slight breeze
I ask, 'have I ever been wed?'

I Am Still Me

How do I know you?
Please explain how
We sat and had a brew
And also some chow

You told me and I listened
Nodded in all the right places
Was someone christened?
My mind is full of faces

I lost my way, who am I
And who are you?
You start to cry
Isn't the sky blue?

I get up and start to walk
You walk with me too
Yet we no longer talk
Then I say, 'Look at that view'

All you see are four blank walls
Yet I am full of smiles
The nurse tells you I have had some falls
And I tell you I have walked miles

You say, 'Goodbye, I will come again soon'
And kiss my cheek gently
I say, 'Look at the moon'
'And have you still got that Bentley'

I watch you as you leave
And turn to the nurse and ask, 'Who was that?'
I keep plucking my sleeve
Then I say, 'Where is the cat?'

Love

They say that the heart is as deep as the ocean
And that true love never runs straight
Sometimes things are set in motion
That can cause a great big weight

The word love is bantered about too readily
And trust is easily broken
Sometimes the line is walked too steadily
And nothing is really spoken

Why can't we say what we mean?
And do what we say
They say that jealousy is usually green
And people usually sway

Always to the negative
Never to the positive
Sometimes people are too sensitive
And usually not talkative

So, trust with what you see
And follow your own gut
Make plenty of time for thee
And never find yourself in that rut

I Am Still Me

Remember how children see the world
Full of colour and joy
See how they laugh every time they twirled
Then how they get coy, when you ask about a boy

The world would be a wondrous place
If we all cared deeply for each other
Accepting each other with grace
And treating each other like our brother

Except for when we are meant to be entwined
Like those soul mates who meet for eternity
And they are never quite confined
And work completely perfectly

Tracey Shorthouse

The Magical Forest

Look how beautiful the forest is as we enter on our walk
Looking around and taking on board the different hues
Listening carefully, we can hear the birds' squawks
And at certain areas near the outskirts, you can see the views

As we traipsed through the forest, following the paths down
We could hear the whisper of trees chattering to each other
In their own language, however we were far enough from the town
As the forest is far from quiet and the leaves did smother

The trunks and those beautiful, gnarled roots going deep into the earth
Shooting sparks of energy to all other living trees and their roots
Bringing life to all, and mother nature starts a new birth
Whilst we press our hands on those trees, we can see new shoots

Of life coming out of every orifice of the 140-acre wood
And as we stand still and listen, we feel we are not alone
As all we hear are creaks and whispers everywhere we stood
We looked up and saw squirrels going to and fro the zone

As we entered the core of the forest, we could hear water rushing
To our amazement and delight, some waterfalls were seen
Some as nature intended and the water was white froth and gushing
Racing over stones but so beautiful clear and clean

Then we saw a hint of colour, amongst the greens and browns
There was a beautiful purple buddleia, with its lovely scent
And a little boys' hideaway, that was nearly round
Leaves covered the roof, and branches had been cut and bent

The rain had started, we could hear the pitter patter
Of the drops hitting the leaves, but we were left dry
So we carried on walking as it really didn't matter
As the trees were so tall, their branches protected us from the sky

We saw some strange fungi, underneath a log
And some money which had been taken by nature
These were in a tree trunk, but nowhere near a bog
And as we carried on, we didn't see any other creature

As we left our magical forest or 140-acre wood
We gave thanks to the trees for their shelter
Because it was only fair and we knew that we could
And at least we had rain and we were cool, and did not swelter

Tracey Shorthouse

My Garden

Look at my garden, see how it grows
When the rain falls, and the sun really glows
The flowers with their buds held tightly together
Suddenly peel open to colour so splendour

The birds swoop down to grab plump worms
And to snatch juicy berries at every turn
Frogs love the ponds and keep the slugs at bay
The wind catches the reeds and they always want to sway

I love my garden, so magical and bright
It is like a fairy haven and might even have a sprite
Even Casper, has his own perch to sit
Watches the birds as they all like to flit

The sparrows, like mischievous little boys
Hide in the honeysuckle and make a lot of noise
The starlings are a bit like nagging women
They like to go onto the feeder when it starts spinning

The blackbirds with their song so sweet
Still giving their young, the odd little treat
The robin visits just to be nosey
With his red breast that always looks so rosy

I Am Still Me

Casper always sees what we can't or unable to
But at least, I am never truly blue
Maybe he sees the fairies visiting
Maybe we can if we believe and then start listening

To the faint laughter and the flap of wings
Out in the garden amongst all the things
When it is dusk or even night
When we tiptoe around the garden, seeing the light so white

Tracey Shorthouse

Ode to Casper

Once there was a young cat
Who had a bad start in life
Although he could catch a rat
Unfortunately, he had plenty of strife

He was bullied and neglected
When he was a kitten
Which made him feel rejected
Then met a woman who was instantly smitten

She adopted him and his brother
About 10 years ago
And suddenly became their new mother
Then it was all go

It wasn't easy,
And there were a few complications
A couple of times he got wheezy
And she needed a lot of patience

He used to spray and get into scraps
Whereas his brother was always good
He used to be scared of any chaps
And sometimes hid in the wood

I Am Still Me

But love won him over
And he learnt to trust
And he was never a rover
And liked to be fussed

He is always a strange one
Who liked to be kissed
Loves being in the sun
And never usually hissed

Likes having his tummy rubbed
And likes being cuddled
But is never ever snubbed
Or never ever muddled

Unlike his mother who is often so
But he doesn't care
He just goes along with the flow
And knows that he is quite rare

In the fact that he is always chatty
So will always remind her
That he doesn't mind her being scatty
Especially when he is there to purr

So now Casper is eleven
And lives the life he loves
Seth is in heaven
And probably still chases the doves
So, this is the end of my ode
To my beautiful cat
I know I am walking a slow road
But at least I know where I am at.

Tracey Shorthouse

Acceptance

When I tell you what is wrong
What my diagnosis is
Please try and be strong
And please don't ever quiz

Don't feel pity or sorry for me
For it is what it is
Just allow me to be free
And my hair will still be a frizz

I've accepted it now
And I'm getting on with my life
So, won't you please accept it somehow
There doesn't have to be strife

You ask and I tell
As a matter of fact
I won't be going to hell
And I am still slightly cracked

So, don't fret or look concerned
I'm a survivor, don't you know
Don't worry, you will never get burned
And we will never ever come to blows

Tracey Shorthouse

Don't say sorry or look uncomfortable
I know that I'm full of peace
There is no way that I am vulnerable
Cause one day I might go to Greece

So, acceptance is the key
For all long-term conditions
And as I clap my hands with glee
These are now my new missions

So, let me tell you, don't be glum
And to get on with your life
For we can be chums
Amongst the wildlife.

Walking in the Woods

As we walk into the woods
Being like intrepid explorers
Knowing it's surrounded by safe neighbourhoods
Without the normal horrors

Tip toeing through the trees
Seeing the different hues
Being chased by a group of bees
Might cause you to have the blues

Fear not, for I am here
To be your protector
I will lead an ear
As we go through the right sector

Branches and roots spread life
Through the foliage and earth
Wild flowers are quite rife
Causing plants, a brand-new birth

A bird calls out and movement is heard
Into the undergrowth we look
We turn our heads and everything is blurred
And I know you slightly shook

Tracey Shorthouse

Fancy you getting jumpy
Whereas all I felt was serene
But at least we weren't grumpy
Being part of a beautiful scene

Bonnie was oblivious
Enjoying all the smells
Sometimes dogs can make us envious
When they can explore the small dells

We only got lost once
Took a wrong turn
We sighed and felt like a dunce
But then how else do we learn

It's quite nice to go for a walk
Trying not to fall in the mud
And to have our usual talk
And luckily there wasn't a flood

Only a few puddles seen
Which Bonnie tried to jump in
But don't worry, you will soon get her clean
And this makes me want to grin

I Am Still Me

Tracey Shorthouse

The Sensory Garden

Roses are in full bloom, deep red in nature
Making the garden full of a heady scent
The bees extract their pollen
The garden is open to every creature
And time is always wisely spent

The garden is full of colour and texture
Good for those that are sensory deprived
Love in the Mist, and Lamb's Ear are prime examples
As a garden, should provide some pleasure
From the time, you have arrived

There is a trug seen on the pathway
With secateurs, flowers are cut
With precision and care
Beautiful climbers seen on the archway
Occasionally we have to shoo the mutt

The garden is separated into divisions
All the elements, fire, water, earth and air
Are seen and used, the children think its magic
It's always good making these decisions
So, the children won't have a scare

There is also an herb garden potted
Lavender is dried and sachets are made
Mint for the potatoes, and rosemary for the lamb
Manure is sometimes rotted
And o'er yonder beyond is a glade

Birds of all kinds come and visit
As do the frogs in the ponds
There is also an owl, who is all knowing and seeing
But then again, is it?
Sticks can be made into wands

All gardens should be loved by all
There is no room for stress
To breathe and relax once more
Even for the kids who peer over the wall
And for those who want to make a mess

We need to use our senses more
To breathe, look and feel
We take so much for granted
Fall asleep and gently snore
And maybe slowly we can start to heal

Tracey Shorthouse

I Am Still Me

The Pirate Sonnet

Ah Ho! My hearties
Look for my ship
See how she bounders o'er the waves
Fighting the fight

We give chase to those unfortunate souls
Rip, Tear and blow others ships to smithereens
See how they roll
Their masts crumbling under the strain

We look for gold and riches
And rum doesn't go amidst
We sing sea shanties
And we go through the chaos and mayhem

Look at the bosom of the mighty young things
In the bar, our wares are put on display
As we try and outdo our compadres
Through tall tales and stories old

Raucous laughter, shouts and fights
Finish the night on a high
We, the pirates, rule the waves
The king and his men may try to catch us

Tracey Shorthouse

But despite best efforts
We will always win
To rule the waves
Forever and so

The Fortune Teller

Come into my parlour, I am the fortune teller
Let me see, into the crystal ball
I see you like wine from your cellar
And your wife has a beautiful shawl

Please sit and give me a farthing
And I will confide in all
I see that you have a wooden carving
Of an elephant, which stands in your hall

Yes, it's getting clearer now, your life which I can see
Don't be afraid, this is what you wanted
I can see how you got down on one knee
Although at the time you were taunted

By her family, cause back then you had no money
Your temper got the better of you
Even though she was still your honey
You called her mother an old shrew

Please don't get cross, you were intrigued
This is why you visited, isn't it?
I know you are feeling fatigued
Of course, you can always quit

If you want to, you can go
And I will put the scarf back on the ball
But I know you want to know, Joe
Don't forget to give me a call

Hello Joe, Nice to see you again
I knew you would be back
Your face shows some strain
Let me take your mac

Would will it be this time
The ball, cards or runes
Listen to the clock chime
We will have a good afternoon

Don't you think it's peaceful here?
Not too bright for you?
I wonder what you want to hear
Shall I tell you something new?

You like the ball, don't you Joe?
Let me see, you went from nothing
Until you had enough dough
Then you went back, and started loving

Your girl all over again, to prove
To her family that you were worth
It, except they had you removed
And threw you into the earth

Don't get mad at me
I only tell you what I see
Although she did plea
For you, they dragged her away with glee

I Am Still Me

A baby she had, nine months later
A boy by all accounts
Her family called her a traitor
And threw her out, luckily the boy did bounce

But you know all this, don't you?
Cause you found them later on
She was tired and blue
And you saw the boy on the lawn

In the park where you had lunch
You looked for her nearby
As had a hunch
And when she saw you, she sat and cried

You gave her a cuddle and made everything right
By asking her to be your wife
She looked at you, with her eyes quite bright
Knowing that you would give her a good life

And your life was good in part
The boy grew to be a fine man
He had a good heart
And met a girl called Anne

I don't understand why you are here
Your life has been very good
I am not a seer
And I wouldn't tell you even if I could

What is wrong? Let me see
Your wife is gravely ill
I suddenly see a tree
And its lies on a hill

Tracey Shorthouse

This is where she will be buried
As it's her favourite place
Near where you were married
And she will be laid out in lace

I am so sorry, but the future is done
I cannot turn the clocks back
You better go and run
Joe, hurry and make tracks

But remember Joe that love
Ruled your life, and she is your girl
You fitted together like hand in glove
She was your Pearl

Yes, I know that is her name
Don't look so startled
Her family should be ashamed
But you made her eyes sparkle

Live your life and love to your best
Have faith that everything will be fine
Try not to get so stressed
And don't be one to pine!!

Tracey Shorthouse

Wishing

I wish I was an eagle flying over head
I wish I was the sun sweeping away the dark
I wish I was a rose deep as ruby red
Or a tree with a bear rubbing against my bark
I wish……………

I wish I was a blackbird who has a sweet song
I wish I was one of the frogs playing in the pond
I wish I was the wind blowing through so strong
Bending the branches and whistling through the valley beyond
I wish………………

I wish I was a spider weaving a web to catch a fly
I wish I was a rainbow full of beautiful colours
I wish I was the rain coming down from the sky
And helping give life to seedlings and others
I wish……………

I wish I was a fire bringing warmth to those who need it
I wish I was a star shooting across the sky to bring luck
I wish I was a child playing in the sand pit
Or going paddling with the ducks
I wish……………

And most of all I wish I was a child seeing the world with fresh eyes
Without judgement and with much laughter

I Am Still Me

Tracey Shorthouse

AUTUMN

Nights are drawing in
There is a crispness to the air
Leaves drop from the trees in a spin
Dancing with a kind of flair

Leaves crunching neath the feet
Red and golden colours cover the trees
The fields are no longer full of wheat
And there might be more of a breeze

Blackberries growing in the hedges
Apple festivals are the norm
Oxeye daisies grow on the road edges
And no longer do wasps swarm

The robin redbreast comes a calling
Conkers drop from the horse chestnut
And acorns and chestnuts are falling
The squirrels start to store their nuts

The birds start to migrate to somewhere hot
At times, there is a heavy dew
Bulbs are planted into a plot
And we might still see some shrews

Tracey Shorthouse

Rushing

People in cities rush around not looking
Like ants in a colony
Yet, not many lose their footing
As they live in a world of economy

Hustle and bustle seems to be the norm
Yet, I stand still letting it wash over me
They are like bees about to swarm
And all I want to do is be free

From the constraints of life and what is
From the rush of traffic and constant noise
Sometimes life is a constant whizz
With men, women, girls and boys

There is a constant buzzing noise in my head
When I'm in a city or town
That always fills me with dread
And gets me feeling rather down

As I long for the place I call home
With the rolling hills and streams
Where I love to roam
Even in my dreams

I Am Still Me

There is always a sense of peace
And tranquillity, And a feeling of calm
It's nice to see sheep, horses and geese
And give polos and apples out of my palm

Traipsing through the fields with the dog
Picking blackberries and apples as I go
Hoping to miss the creeping fog
But still aiming to bump into my beau

There is no Hustle and bustle in the country
It's a different world, the pace is slower
Sometimes there is a field with one tree
And the verges get done with one man and his mower.

Tracey Shorthouse

The Halloween Party

There was a full moon seen on All Hallows Eve
Over the graveyard on the hill
An old tramp watched at the gate plucking his sleeve
With his bottle of Holston Pils

He was waiting with bated breath
Knowing that the spirits would rise
There is no such thing as death
Amongst those who were really wise

For when it's Halloween
That is the time to party
Who will you be witch? or queen?
Drinking and laughing hearty

Parties go on everywhere
Alive and dead both go
Spirits might indeed have a flair
And they also have a glow

So, the spirits took turns to rise
From their graves, the tramp saw
It was good to have clear skies
Even the tramp was in awe

I Am Still Me

For there was the grey lady
Gliding across calling to the others
Already there was a faint melody of Rosie 'O' Grady
And suddenly there were the Grimm Brothers

With their stories, sitting on their tomb stones
And the Borley Rectory nun was seen praying
Some of the spirits were hitting their bones
Making music with their own sort of playing

A strange combination on this eerie night
Dancing and playing til dawn
Then silence reigned once more on this sight
When the birds started singing on this morn

The tramp had joined in with the drinking
And had fallen asleep at the end
Once he awoke, he couldn't stop blinking
As there stood in front of him was an old girl friend

She tipped her head sideways and gave him a smile
She blew him a kiss and started to fade
He wished he had got her down the aisle
But he was too late and afraid

He was sad when she died
And started to drink and let himself go
He never really cried
But now they started to flow
He realised that the reason he saw the party
Was so that he could let go of the past
He realised that he had to be a smarty
Pants, to get back his life at last

Tracey Shorthouse

Our Nan

Our nan was called Joyce Agnes
The second name she absolutely loathed
But her life was never filled with sadness
And John was her betrothed

They had a happy life together
And a daughter, Anne, was born
Nan loved to grow heather
And used to like to walk through fields of corn

She always used to say that her life
Was like a suet pudding
As she didn't like any strife
And she didn't like cooking

However, she always made a nice roast beef
Casseroles, dumplings, and rock cakes too
She always thought herself as the chief
Of us three and you

Nan loved her garden and the pond
Her friends and the hub
There she felt a special bond
And loved going into the pub

Tracey Shorthouse

Nan loved frogs, dogs and cats
And her last cat was Beanie
She didn't really mind the rats
But her tipple certainly wasn't a martini

She liked a Baileys or two
And occasionally white wine spritzer
Milky coffee was her favourite brew
Although she wasn't a great mixer

Her favourite colour was blue
But she really didn't like green
Nan used to like the odd view
And really liked the Queen

Nan used to potter about
And most of all enjoy the day
At times, she used to pout
If she didn't get her way

I feel sad that she has gone
But 90 is a good age
But at least she is with her John
And has gone on to the next stage

Christmas Thoughts

Children's faces light up with elation
Holly growing with berries so red
Reindeers prancing in front of the sleigh
Ice on the floor where people fear to tread

Santa coming down the chimney
Turkey eaten with some peas
Mistletoe hung where kisses are shared
Angel sitting on top of the tree

Snow may fall making a magical land
Tradition brings a lot of joy
Holidays bring families together
Oranges enjoyed by little boys

Unwrap those individual presents
Goodwill spread to all around us
Happiness is spread worldwide
Toys are shared without much fuss

Season Greetings to all our friends and family.

Tracey Shorthouse

Dear Santa

Dear Santa, this letter I write
Since I am four
Please can I have a bike?
Or a spinning top, which whistles when spun
Or a doll, cause all these would make life fun

Dear Santa, this letter I write
Since I am ten
Please can I have a kite?
To fly up with the birds, and be free
Oh, can you please hear my plea

Dear Santa, this letter I write
Now I am 20
Please can I have my own knight
One who will bring me roses, and make me happy
And stop me from being lonely and snappy

Dear Santa, this letter I write
Now I am 30
My fella and I had a fight
Please can you bring him back
So, we can both make a pact

I Am Still Me

Dear Santa, this letter I write
Now I am 40
Please know our plight
For a child, we wish for more than not
Please make it more than a single thought

Dear Santa, this letter I write
I am now 70
I am asking for a winter so white
So, the grandchildren can see a magical land
Of make believe, one that is planned

Dear Santa, this letter I write
I am now nearly 90
And don't want to give my family a fright
So, let me fall asleep, so peace will come
And I can float away, from life which is glum

Dear Santa, all I ask that is left of me
A gift for my family and friends
To go out on a shopping spree
To live, laugh and be happy
But never ever be scrappy.

Tracey Shorthouse

The Christmas Fairy

Matilda was flying overhead when she
Spied a young boy sitting by a stream
He looked so sad as he peered into the water
Then at the corner of his eye, he saw a beam

Of such beautiful light, he glanced up
And there was a fairy sitting on a stone
She was smoothing her green skirts over her knees
When she looked up and told him that he was never alone

Her hair was golden like a ray of sunshine
Entwined with a sprig of holly and a berry to match
The redness of her top, her eyes seemed to sparkle
In the light, so mesmerized was he that he nearly didn't quite catch

What she said. He looked at her in awe and went quiet
Matilda tilted her head and asked, 'Why are you so sad, dear?'
Her voice was like a musical melody
So, soothing and relaxing to be near

He asked her who she was first and she replied
Why I am the Christmas fairy, the granter of all wishes
He told her that his name was Tommy, that he got lost
From his family, saw the stream and all the fishes

Now the sun was starting to set, and he wanted to go home
Matilda told him that all he had to do was follow her light
And she would lead him back to his parents
For she was a magical fairy sprite

All you have to do is have faith
Trust and believe in magic
You will soon be back with your family
So, stop looking so tragic

When Matilda flew up into the air, Tommy could see a tiny light
He watched and followed carefully so not to fall
Then heard his parents call to him
He ran into their arms trying not to bawl

'Where have you been? We have been so worried'
Asked his family. Tommy tried to tell of the fairy
And the help she gave him, and of the stream that he found
His parents didn't really believe and spoke of a woman called Mary

Who they were visiting later that day. As they walked away chatting
Matilda sat on the branch of a tree
She smiled as she watched them leave
Knowing that children will always be free

In their hearts and heads for they will always believe
In Magic, in Santa Claus, in elves and of course fairies
Some adults do as well, for these are special people
Who take care of the flowers, plants and cherries.

Lightning Source UK Ltd.
Milton Keynes UK
UKOW03f1009210217
294853UK00001B/3/P